G000066528

CHINESE ASTROLOGY

ANCIENT WISDOM
FOR THE NEW AGE

CHINESE
ASTROLOGY

Chung Li

NEW
HOLLAND

First published in 1997 by
New Holland (Publishers) Ltd
London • Cape Town • Sydney • Singapore

24 Nutford Place, London W1H 6DQ, UK

80 McKenzie Street, Cape Town 8000, South Africa

3/2 Aquatic Drive, Frenchs Forest, NSW 2086, Australia

Distributed by Sterling Publishing Company, Inc
387 Park Avenue South, New York, NY 10016

Distributed in Canada by Sterling Publishing
c/o Canadian Manda Group, One Atlantic Avenue, Suite 105,
Toronto, Ontario, Canada M6K 3E7

ISBN 1 85368 950 5 (hb)

DESIGNED AND EDITED BY
Complete Editions
40 Castelnau
London SW13 9RU

EDITORIAL DIRECTION: Yvonne McFarlane
EDITOR: Michèle Brown
DESIGNER: Peter Ward

Reproduction by Modern Age Repro House Ltd, Hong Kong
Printed and bound in Singapore by Tien Wah Press Pte Ltd

CONTENTS

ACROSS THE MILLENIA

Chinese Astrology is the oldest known form of prediction, though it should more correctly be seen as a form of philosophical guidance. Chinese astrologers were concerned with the whole person, not single events which may or may not happen in the future. The ancients charted the heavens with perceptive wisdom, using readings of the night sky to make their philosophical pronouncements.

Events in the life of the peoples of the early civilisations of the Yellow River Valley were subject to the whims of the heavens. Floods, storms, hail, blistering sun and terrible drought were all accorded to the movement of the stars and planets. In the earliest recorded documents particular events are correlated to particular heavenly happenings. An eclipse might appear to coincide with a flood and so on. As these were recorded over the centuries, they formed a huge body of wisdom from which the cyclical nature of the universe was perceived. In one astrological treatise alone there are over 2,500 recorded happenings, related to causes.

The sages of the Shang Dynasty (1500-1100BC) who recorded and interpreted these events were thought to have divinatory powers and soon found themselves in positions of political power. They knew as much about the movements of the heavenly bodies as they did about the psychology of the people who toiled in the fields. They used that knowledge to evolve a whole social system which would eventually be codified by such eminent philosophers as Confucius in his *Analects* and in the works of Lao-tze.

They thought that if their known universe was of a cyclical nature, so was the nature of man. To him they assigned a perfect lifespan of sixty years, which were divided by the five elements – wood, fire, earth, metal and water – to give the twelve earthly branches, which would evolve into the twelve animal years. Each of these was then divided into lunar months, again with specific attributes.

The celestial bodies, first recorded over four millenia ago, still follow the same heavenly paths overhead, tracing out the same ancient wisdom for us today.

YIN AND YANG

The basic concept which underlies all Chinese philosophy, medicine and astrology is that of Yin and Yang. Together they make up Qi, the essential life force. In the Yellow Emperor's *Canon of Internal Medicine*, it is claimed that Yin and Yang constitute the basic principle of the whole universe. The years and months of the Chinese calendar have Yin and Yang aspects, as do organs of the body.

Yin has connotations of softness, darkness, coldness and wetness, its symbol being a mountain topped by a cloud. Yang has connotations of hardness, brightness, heat and dryness, its symbol being a sun with shining rays. Perfect health or perfect peace of mind depend on an

equal balance of Yin and Yang. In Chinese astrology a Yin year might modify a Yang month and vice versa. A Yin month in a Yin year might presage problems, similarly with Yang. These have been taken into account in the Mansions of the Moon readings.

HEAVENLY PALACES

The Twelve Divisions of the Chinese calendar are based on the ancient belief that the universe was 3,600 years old, divided into twelve, sixty-year cycles. For centuries these divisions were simply referred to as the Twelve Branches, but slowly they were ascribed the characteristics of the twelve animals. It was thought for years that they had been so named by the Chinese in antiquity, but recent studies of ancient manuscripts suggest that the names were taken to China from Turkey or Central Asia. There is no mention of the names in the texts of the Han Dynasty (200 BC–AD 200) when astrological studies were at their peak and they may have been used first as recently as AD 800. Many of the characteristics attributed to animals by the Chinese differ from Western ideas. The Snake can be a power for good, as can the Rat, wheras both have unpleasant connotations in the Western mind.

THE YEAR OF THE RAT

1912 1924 1936 1948 1960
1972 1984 1996 2008 2020

The Rat personality is charming, appealing, clever, quick witted and sociable. It also hoards and wastes. Rats, together with mice (after whom this year is sometimes named), were always considered wise creatures in Chinese mythology. Scurrying around in the dark they were also thought to be creatures with occult powers. The rat was regarded as a noble creature, exploring far and away to discover the wider world, so Rats have a natural curiosity, with an inquisitive nature. They want to know the how, why and wherefore of everything.

Those born in the Year of the Rat have a way with words, spoken or written. Wit falls naturally from lips or pen, yet they have a practical bent too and can take most tasks in hand with natural ease.

As night creatures, Rats are great socialisers, rarely turning down a party invitation. They like the fast track of life and are great risk-takers. They'll gamble on anything in life, at the gaming tables, in love or in business. They have incurably romantic natures. As the first sign in the New Year, they enjoy feasting and enjoying the fruits of the hard work which went into the previous harvest.

All this feverish social activity hints at underlying insecurity. Perhaps Rats secretly fear that one day they will not be loved, or they will not have the means to finance their favoured lifestyle. This can lead to stocking up larders too full, having multiple savings accounts and mentally having several affairs, just in case . . .

The Rat month heralds a new year, which is why they are endlessly optimistic and happiest just before midnight in anticipation of the good things to come.

THE YEAR OF THE OX

1913 1925 1937 1949 1961
1973 1985 1997 2009 2021

The Ox is dependable, above all else. Related to the land, the ox in many folklores is a symbol of fertility and fruitfulness. Appearing early in the year the Chinese Ox is an augury of the impending arrival of Spring.

But dependability has a dark side. People born in the Year of the Ox can be stubborn and sullen. Once their mind is made up nothing will change it. They will continue ploughing the same furrow, oblivious to any outside influence or distraction. They are naturally blinkered. This same determination can also lead to possessiveness which can achieve the strength of a major obsession.

Ox people are much more intelligent than they are given credit for. An affinity with the great outdoors makes them aware of the fate of the environment. They are great home lovers, much in need of a stable base to suit their overall personality, and great believers in the stability of family life.

In business and friendship they supply boundless strength, great endurance and total allegiance. Used to being yoked, they are great team workers, with complete reliability, guaranteed to pull their weight.

After deep winter, the Ox can see spring around the corner and starts planning for it in the usual methodical manner, mulling over the plans late into the night while gathering energy for the following day.

THE YEAR OF THE TIGER

1914 1926 1938 1950 1962
1974 1986 1998 2010 2022

Tigers are competitive in the extreme and brave to the point of rashness. They are charismatic and they know it. Though they like to hunt alone, they consider themselves natural leaders. They are out to do something for the greater good, but like their efforts to be noticed. They think themselves naturally superior and in any army would consider themselves the automatic choice to be General Commanding, a position they would fill with honour and dignity.

The Tiger means well, but behind the radiant smile lies a fiercesome bite. The sense of composure belies the energy which is there to be set free. Tigers are always at the ready to attack. The will for conquest is never dormant for long; conquest in business or personal relationships is all important.

In spite of being a high achiever, capable of juggling

with several projects at once, the Tiger's lair, the home, is very important. A Tiger has to feel safe somewhere, as it feels menaced everywhere else. That it might be menacing to others does not usually cross the Tiger's mind. It is taken as natural that a Tiger should be in charge. The home will inevitably live up to the Tiger's style, being beautifully furnished, to the point of ostentation.

The Tigers' negative qualities arise out of the proliferation of talents they possess. Their power proliferates as well, sometimes with overbearing results.

Tigers thrive in the early spring when they can look

for new territories to conquer. During the long winter nights beforehand they conserve their energy.

THE YEAR OF THE RABBIT

1915 1927 1939 1951 1963
1975 1987 1999 2011 2023

Rabbits have curious contradictions in their character. They are wildly gregarious, but when in party situations can remain aloof, as though observing the revels. It suggests that they are nervous of getting involved, as they will do anything to avoid a confrontation. But while observing they are also collecting information for a good gossip later. They are good readers of body language and hidden relationships.

Rabbits are prolific breeders, but not necessarily sensual. Adding to the family comes first, for the family is very important. Though their instinct is to roam, for they are intensely inquisitive, they are never happier than when scurrying back home. Home will quite likely be inhabited for life. Upheavals are not for them.

The Rabbit's desire to avoid confrontation and conflict, to run rather than fight, makes for a wily mind, with an instinctive intelligence to get out of any sticky situation.

Rabbits, like cats, are constantly preening themselves and enjoy the luxury of being pampered at a health farm or beautician's salon. Rabbits, like squirrels, are hoarders, preferably of newly-bought merchandise. 'Shop 'til you drop' is the Rabbit's motto, with no thought for the morrow.

Rabbits are good friends and business partners as they believe in long-term relationships, based on steady mutual growth.

Spring suits the Rabbit, when new shoots are appearing and there is energy in the air. Very early morning sees them early-rising, when they can go out and about unobserved.

THE YEAR OF THE DRAGON

1916 1928 1940 1952 1964
1976 1988 2000 2012 2024

The Dragon which crossed the Chinese skies represented the passage of time, marking anything from auspicious events to the menstrual cycle. It was exotic and blessed with occult powers and regarded as a vital force. Unlike threatening Western dragons, the Chinese Dragon is a helpful creature, ruling the elements of weather. And so Dragon people are in a position to influence events, through their intuitive understanding of almost any situation.

This influence is not always for the best, but at least something is being done. Occasionally a complete lack of realism will affect the result. Dragons believe in themselves so much that they can fool themselves into believing that they are infallible. They can be unmethodical in their need for action at any price. They like starting projects or relationships, but their youth-like impetuosity can send them off in other directions before anything comes to fruition.

Underneath their out-
ward show of bravado,
there is a shadow of
insecurity, which explains
the need for everything
to always look good on
the outside, whether it is a brave
face or smart new clothes.

Channelling their energy is a
full-time job for Dragons, they never let
up. When things don't work, tempers fray and friends may
suffer. Keeping an even keel is a good goal for the Dragon.

Dragons like early summer, when the fruits of spring
are evident. Something is
happening, so Dragons
are happy. Early
morning suits them
well, with a whole day
of activity to look
forward to.

THE YEAR OF THE SNAKE

1917 1929 1941 1953 1965
1977 1989 2001 2013 2025

Snakes are a collection of contradictions. They are wise and naive, they are prudent and prudish, they are profligate and possessive. They seem quiet and passive, but are coiled for sudden strikes. In Chinese folklore the Snake is often associated with female temptresses or goddesses, with their ability to hypnotize and charm.

The seemingly placid nature of the Snake, lying in wait, suggests patience and an ability to choose the right moment to act, particularly if they can control events from afar. They can also endure long periods of apparent inactivity, but the time is not wasted. They are planning their next strike. Intellectualising is a trait of most Snakes. They gather information and intelligence from every possible source, accumulating it for the right moment. This does not fetter their imagination and they can come up with intensely original ideas, particularly in the arts. The constant use of the brain can sometimes lead to mild instability and unbalanced judgments. Mastery of all the facts does not mean that the answer to a problem is automatically right. But the Snake will believe it to be so.

Snakes do not like to go far from home and need companionship. When they do venture forth it will be for some creative enterprise. They love art, but there is a calculation in their collecting of yet more knowledge. Do they instinctively like a painting or simply think that they should know about the painting?

Snakes like the peak of summer, when they can absorb the sun, just as they absorb facts and figures. They are late risers, stirring themselves long after others have set off for work. Lying in bed late conserves their energies, as they are somewhat hypochondriacal and constantly believe they are of delicate health.

THE YEAR OF THE HORSE

1918 1930 1942 1954 1966
1978 1990 2002 2014 2026

Horses were highly honoured in China. Horse people are sociable, sporting, hard-working and widely travelled. Their all-round abilities can give them strong prejudices, a strong streak of selfishness and not a little intolerance. After all, if they can do so much they must be right, mustn't they?

Horses have endless vitality and energy. Their surging power can drive them to do anything, which in turn seems to bring them endless luck. Life is a continuous game to be won, a game in which the Horse is always on the offensive. No defensive games are played and few games are lost. It is significant that when a Horse rears, the movement is both offensive and defensive.

Fortunately the Horse's towering ambition does not exclude close friendships, for many of the Horse's battles are fought on behalf of others. In spite of individualistic qualities, Horses make good team-mates, if they can fight the urge to be captain every time. They like to play a broad game, leaving the details to others. Their strength is both mental and physical, with brute strength often winning through. This makes them extremely practical and good at manual jobs and tasks around the house, although not heavy labouring.

Achieving success so easily can make Horses annoyed with themselves when things *don't* work out as planned. They get just as annoyed with others if they can't match their achievements. When things aren't going right it is often because Horses charge ahead, looking into the distance, missing the immediate details. Horses don't take their time about anything.

Horses love high summer, when their energy is at its peak, just as they like midday when the sun is high and the time to refresh their energies approaches.

THE YEAR OF THE RAM

1919 1931 1943 1955 1967
1979 1991 2003 2015 2027

Rams are nature's conservatives. They dislike disorder, want everything filed in its proper place and believe there is a method for doing everything. Unfortunately they sometimes cannot find the correct method and suffer from mental anguish. Consistency comes high on their list of values. No rash promises or ambitious aims – all must be completely realistic and achievable.

These qualities make Rams seem boring, but they mean well. They want things to run like clockwork, and not just for their own good. Friends come first and they will organize and arrange business, parties and introductions for their benefit. Sometimes this help can seem like interference or criticism, but it is all meant for the best, with little or no self-interest.

Ram people do not behave as the animal itself is often portrayed. They bide their time, playing a waiting game for the perfect moment to act. They do not charge ahead regardless, however tempting the incentive may be.

Rams aren't the most inspirational of people. Ideas don't spring naturally from a Ram's brain. Results are achieved by research and calculation, but are often none the worse for that. True inspiration is often stifled through a search for the *perfect* solution rather than a *working* solution. Such thoroughness can often lead to delays, which in turn can lead to a dimming of enlightenment.

Home life is important to Rams, not just for a restful background, but as something to be proud of and to show to others. Social life is limited. Rams would prefer to give parties rather than go to them. They enjoy watching other people enjoy themselves as a result of their efforts.

Rams enjoy the late summer, placidly waiting for the fruits of their labour to come forth and be harvested. A favourite time of day is after a late lunch when energy is garnered to go on to greater efforts.

THE YEAR OF THE MONKEY

1920 1932 1944 1956 1968
1980 1992 2004 2016 2028

Monkeys are always on the go, mentally and physically.
They are audacious and inventive, agile and hyperactive.
Such is the activity, that periods in a manic-depressive state
may occur, leading to nagging insecurity. Expending such
energy has to take its toll in the end.

But such doubts are drowned in a sea of irrepressible,
lively fun, as the Monkey leads everyone on a merry
dance. At times sexually teasing, at others manipulative, the
Monkey's actions are invariably intended for good and
never for their own advantage.

However crazy Monkeys may seem,
they know precisely what they
are doing. They also have a
child-like ability to play games on
people and then innocently
give the whole game away. At

times they may seem cunning, approaching life with a devil-may-care attitude, in the belief that they will always get what they want. Most times they do, because other people are happy to indulge them in return for the endless pleasure they give.

Mercurial is the key word for Monkeys. They are the world's fidgets, interfering with other people's lives, almost always with positive effects.

As autumn falls, Monkeys find the crisp air even more energizing, and as afternoon comes to an end, with a hint of warmth still in the air, Monkeys take advantage and get up to yet more tricks.

THE YEAR OF THE ROOSTER

1925 1933 1945 1957 1969
1981 1993 2005 2017 2029

The Rooster is alert to new ideas, problems on the horizon, other people's problems and chances to lead. As leaders Roosters can be remarkably selfless, which is the opposite of much of a Rooster's character. As employers they can be hard taskmasters, but they always have the best interests of their employees at heart. But the business will

have been started out of pure self-interest, which is a motivating factor in many of the Rooster's actions.

If anything the Rooster can suffer from a dose of over-confidence. This leads to crowing once too often about their own achievements, which other people may find off-putting.

Being aware of your own worth is one thing, constantly harping upon it, another. Abrasive and competitive qualities also irritate others, but are often used to good effect. The Rooster wants to get on with things. Getting there is important, the means of getting there a minor irritation.

Roosters love display. They stand out at parties by extravagance of appearance and behaviour. They love feasts and celebrations, which they are able to indulge in through their relative prosperity. Roosters are achievers, their easy confidence giving them the ability to win most races, at the office, at play or in personal relationships.

Roosters are at peak performance in the late afternoon, and the later months of the year when the sun is setting and the harvest is in. These are the moments when the Rooster can sit back and relax, before heralding another busy day.

THE YEAR OF THE DOG

1922 1934 1946 1958 1970
1982 1994 2006 2018 2030

In all cultures the dog is the symbol of total loyalty and friendship. For the Chinese protection is a key word. Dogs are never happier than when prowling around the house or office, making sure that things are safe for others. They are not afraid to attack if a friend is threatened in any way. They get involved, often without thinking through the consequences to themselves. What they want is a result *now* and not long discussions or negotiations stretching into the weeks ahead. Getting things done is equally important. When not on the go, Dogs appear placid, but in fact, they have restless souls and are planning to go a'roving, or possibly anticipating problems.

Honesty and straightforwardness are hallmarks of all Dogs. These qualities make few enemies and attract long lasting friendship from others. They also make the showing of feelings very easy and unembarrassing.

Optimism is a prime quality of Dogs. Life is one big opportunity, but optimism, when overdone, can lead to disappointments, as can overconfidence deriving from the passionate friendship of others. Sometimes friends are not what they seem, so it is good for Dogs to occasionally lie down, look around and take stock of people and possessions.

Late in the year, as winter draws on, the Dog does not relax. While other animals hibernate, and as night falls, the Dog alone remains awake and aware.

THE YEAR OF THE PIG

1923 1935 1947 1959 1971
1983 1995 2007 2019 2031

The Pig ends the annual cycle, but celebrates the idea of impending rebirth. The New Year is imminent and new horizons beckon.

Contentment is a key word in the Pig's vocabulary. You take the world as you find it, no matter how creative and intelligent you are. And creative and intelligent you are, no matter what the common impression of the Pig is. The innate goodness of the Pig is shown by the way the intelligence is used; often for the benefit of others. Pigs are selfless in the extreme, generous to others, whilst not over-spending on themselves.

A Pig's social life can flourish. You join in and give your all, but in the end you like to come home. Herein lies a problem. Homecoming and settling down can become a little obsessive, at times to the point of inducing deep melancholia. The family is important. Meeting regularly around the dinner table for family meals or pow-wows is an cherished part of the Pig's routine.

At the end of the year the Pig presides over the seasonal festivities, usually late in the evening, while deep down pondering the future.

MANSIONS
OF THE MOON

Having discovered your basic character traits using the
animal years, these can be modified by the patterns
suggested by the Mansions of the Moon, the twelve lunar
divisions that make up each Chinese year, which changes
in length from year to year. To find your Moon month
consult the chart on pages 60-63. For example, if you were
born on March 21st, 1940, you will see that the 2nd Moon
starts on March 9th and the 3rd Moon on April 4th.
Therefore you were born in the 2nd Moon. The Chinese
New Year falls on the 1st of the 1st Moon, which is usually
at the end of January or the beginning of February.

The suggestions that follow are based on the broad
effects derived from the Yin and Yang forces of each
month, in relation to those of each year. A Yin Moon may
well soften the characteristics of a Yang year and vice versa.

YEAR OF THE RAT

1ST MOON: Sensitive and restless, you enjoy initiating controversial new ideas. **2ND:** Introversion may make you seem indifferent. Look outward. **3RD:** Anything to be different is your trait. Try agreeing. **4TH:** You stick with your ideas, positive or negative. Be flexible. **5TH:** An artistic temperament runs deep. Express emotions through it. **6TH:** Like Leos, you enjoy the good things of life, and like letting people know it. Your enthusiasm makes you a good salesman. **7TH:** If you are a prevaricator, don't worry. All's well in the long-term. **8TH:** You have everything and this may bring your downfall. Brains, looks and good fortune aren't everything. **9TH:** See the wider world and leave the details which concern you to others. **10TH:** Don't expect to be lucky every time. Gambles in life don't always come off. **11TH:** Your interest in everything can produce a butterfly mind. Concentrate. **12TH:** As the Year of the Ox approaches, avoid a tendency to stubbornness. Stay a smooth Rat.

YEAR OF THE OX

1st Moon: The departing Rat makes you less stubborn and more self-confident. **2nd:** Your intense creativity can lead to introspection making relationships difficult. People can let you down as a result. **3rd:** Not a great mixer. Remember things aren't as bad as they seem. **4th:** Deep thinking leads to lack of action. Come to conclusions. **5th:** Your quick wit is used too often to cover slip-ups. **6th:** A month favouring the young. Enjoy it to the full. Grow up gracefully. **7th:** A cool exterior conceals your hyperactive, creative, mind. **8th:** Serious socializing conceals a home-lover. Work at it. **9th:** Easily taken advantage of, your generosity will be rewarded.

10th: Self-reliance suggests you would enjoy being self-employed. **11th:** Power-lovers abound under this Moon. But this doesn't make you any less good and thoughtful a friend to many. **12th:** More power-lovers, loners, over-sensitive to criticism.

YEAR OF THE TIGER

1st Moon: You are more reserved than most Tigers through the influence of the Ox, but you still have a tendency to flamboyance. Settle down – eventually. **2nd:** Your extreme reactions to people or events makes you too forth-right. **3rd:** Keep an eye on yourself. Are you too generous, too daring or too loving? **4th:** Your infectious personality cheers up others, but do be faithful. **5th:** Are you gregarious or do you prefer your own company? Or do you swing from one to the other? Opposites can often be reconciled in one person. **6th:** Out of the doldrums, calm will eventually descend. **7th:** Straight dealing will ensure success in your community. **8th:** Doing your own thing is artistically productive. **9th:** Your love of beauty may make you seem superficial, but you aren't. **10th:** Plough your own straight furrow, ignoring criticism or problems. **11th:** Your constant pursuit of ideals and ideas depletes your mental and physical energy. Pace yourself. **12th:** Your supreme self-confidence can make you oblivious to the jealous tendencies of others. Press on, you don't mean ill.

YEAR OF THE RABBIT

1st Moon: Following the Tiger gives you that extra confidence. Plunge ahead with your plans which are usually straightforward and forthright. **2nd:** Stop scampering and take time to consider and discuss projects. **3rd:** You will inherit more than property. A decisive mind is as much good. **4rd:** Others feel protective towards you. Accept this with good grace. **5th:** Your tendency to indecision causes worries. Share them to ease them. **6th:** Your conformist exterior hides a hedonist inside. Let it out sometimes. **7th:** You stir it up and get things done, in politics, business, family and the creative world, from architecture to fashion. **8th:** Ever the optimist, your innate confidence keeps things on the go, even when you are happily charging down a blind alley. **9th:** Like Scorpios you have a tendency to hoard, to the point of obsession. **10th:** Essentially private, you excel at solo sports. Life's team games aren't for you. **11th:** You'll try anything to get what you want, but not to the point of betrayal. **12th:** Approaching Dragon gives you the energy to succeed in almost any venture.

YEAR OF THE DRAGON

1ST MOON: The preceding Rabbit makes you more introspective, but this does produce a stream of original ideas, not taken seriously at first. **2ND:** As you sail through life, your composure gives no hint of inner turmoil. **3RD:** Your tendency to live life to the full, indulging others emotionally and financially is matched by your physical exuberance. **4TH:** What you see is what you get if you are born under this Moon.

5TH: Concentration on the job in hand means you can overcome many obstacles. **6TH:** A flurry of talk and creativity follows your whirlwind through life. **7TH:** Your talent to inspire confidence and trust is a boon to others. **8TH:** Logic prevails. Everything has to have a concrete goal for you. **9TH:** With your head in the clouds, your ideas seem a bit airy-fairy to others, but you know that out of dreams have come many great inventions, books and paintings. **10TH:** Your placid exterior misleads. Beneath there is a sleeping dragon ready to strike. **11TH:** Determination is the least of your worries. Your will to win is notorious. **12TH:** Forthcoming Snake gives you a cool exterior, but a Dragon's warmth lies within.

YEAR OF THE SNAKE

1st Moon: Amassing information can depress. Knowledge is power but too much is dangerous. **2nd:** Don't keep everything to yourself, it worries friends and colleagues. **3rd:** It is better work for yourself, through your ambition, but don't become over-confident. Take a more relaxed approach to life. **4th:** Don't think of yourself quite so much. It will create a closed world. **5th:** Your eye for treasures in all fields is wholly admirable. Cultivate it. **6th:** Your procrastination can be positive, suggesting a cautious mind. Apply this to help other, less confident, people. **7th:** Leo's influence makes Snakes born in this Moon unusually active. Take advantage and make conquests. **8th:** Your natural aggression and over-confidence can bring surprises, not all of them favourable. **9th:** An outgoing character brings fortunate relationships in work and at home. **10th:** Don't repress things, which is your natural instinct. Let go for once. **11th:** Use your talents for communicating and social organizing to best effect. **12th:** Arriving Horse suggests being more direct and adventurous.

YEAR OF THE HORSE

1st Moon: Your brilliant career, which started early, can only continue.

2nd: Try working with people, instead of always doing your own thing.

3rd: Spring's here. Enjoy it. Find new friends. You may need them.

4th: Intellect will out and the results show your artistic talents. **5th:** Resist the urge to show off the fruits of your labours. **6th:** Try not to hop from person to person in a search for security. **7th:** A lucky Moon, make the most of it. Self-reliance will pay off handsomely. **8th:** Try not to indulge yourself quite so much, though you do temper this tendency with generosity of pocket and spirit. **9th:** Keep your head and play a waiting game to succeed in spite of setbacks, some of which are of your own making, largely a result of unthinking haste. **10th:** Find an easier way of communicating with people. Open up. **11th:** When times are hard use your capacity for analysis to solve problems. **12th:** Forthcoming Ram softens your headstrong tendencies and will result in leisurely success rather than galloping failure.

YEAR OF THE RAM

1st Moon: Make the most of this period of heightened inner power. Win games, boardroom battles. Have fun. **2nd:** Accept that upheavals sometimes do have to happen and don't worry about them. **3rd:** Cerebral activity predominates your life, but don't let it take over completely. **4th:** You want the best of everything and,

being a sensual and social person, will probably get it. **5th:** Keep talking and keep mixing. This is your natural environment. **6th:** Be a little outgoing. Your deep thoughts keep you from other people. **7th:** Wanting the best in life, people or possessions is no bad thing when the intentions behind the desire are as correct as yours. **8th:** Try not to worry so much. People are not out to deceive quite as much as you think. **9th:** Your serious exterior hides a serious interior, concerned that you can't control everything. **10th:** Things work out eventually for you, even though confusion appears to reign. **11th:** Being a home-lover is no bad thing. Don't worry if home is not perfect. **12th:** Frivolous Monkey arriving relieves the usual work pressures.

YEAR OF THE MONKEY

1ST MOON: Use your particular charm to get people organized. It's appreciated. **2ND:** Curb a tendency to hoard and collect. It could become an obsession. **3RD:** Channel energies into making the most of your employment. **4TH:** Try to avoid being clever-clever. You can win with perfectly conventional methods. Straightforwardness is not a sin. **5TH:** Don't be afraid to trumpet your achievements. Being proud is one thing. Being insufferably vain, another. **6TH:** Like Leos, those born under this Moon have supreme confidence which can ensure they make it in almost any field. **7TH:** Use your communication skills to best effect, be it in politics or entertainment. **8TH:** You often don't see the wood for the trees. Ignore a few irrelevent details. **9TH:** A vibrant time of year. Try an innocent's approach to life. See everything anew. **10TH:** Time to focus your butterfly mind. Be organized to achieve aims. **11TH:** Your calm, cool approach to business, as a manager or organizer, is a true help to others. **12TH:** Resist urges to be on the move, from job to job or person to person.

YEAR OF THE ROOSTER

1st Moon: Usually agressive, at this time of year this tendency is softened and you can listen rather than crow. **2nd:** Sitting at home alone, planning and organizing, may cause troubles.

3rd: Springtime encourages the starting of new projects. Go ahead. **4th:** Get out and about. Your tendency to brood, albeit on scholarly matters, can lead to problems in later life. **5th:** A time of extremes. Let the forces guide you, right or wrong. **6th:** Let the wamth of the sun kindle those ideas you want to happen.

7th: Imperfections can be to your advantage. Under this Moon you are probably much less self-centred than many Roosters.

8th: The influence of the 7th Moon lingers on. You listen, not instruct, and know that there is such a thing as modesty.

9th: Another calm exterior, hiding the fact that you are paddling madly underneath. **10th:** Collect, collect, collect. This habit won't go away, so enjoy it. **11th:** Yin and Yang are in balance, so achievements will be gained by careful work. **12th:** The loyal Dog approaches so your friendly character is strengthened.

YEAR OF THE DOG

1ST MOON: Look to the future and resist temptations to live for the day. **2ND:** Usually loyal, this Moon can suggest a change of character brought about by forces beyond your control. **3RD:** Your persistence will produce results in fields of communication.
4TH: Feel good that you can make other people feel good. It is to your benefit. **5TH:** If colleagues think you conceited, don't worry. They resent your self-confidence, which is not of an over-bearing nature. You are as good as you think you are. **6TH:** Brainy, but not pedantic, you can get things done where others have failed. **7TH:** You should be basking in the summer sun, but inner problems find you unable to press ahead with work. **8TH:** Don't be hard on others or expect them to be as perfect as yourself.
9TH: If you feel that you are being subverted, you may be right. Take action. **10TH:** Keep your wits about you. Influences from the previous Moon are still active, suggesting that untruths may

be circulating. **11TH:** If a new hand of friend-ship is offered, take it. Friends are always good news. **12TH:** Pig's benign influence tells you not to bound about aimlessly. Work consistently.

YEAR OF THE PIG

1st Moon: Expect success, but through your earnest application, rather than luck. **2nd:** Luck abounds, but don't take it for granted and become over-confident. **3rd:** Sort through the myriad of ideas you have. You may not have the mental or physical resources to see them all through. **4th:** Make the most of your youth. Middle-age problems will be resolved in later years. **5th:** Be more trustful, against your natural instincts. **6th:** A little prevarication is no bad thing, as once you've made up your mind you have definitely made up your mind. **7th:** Amongst the hurly-burly you can create, real achievements are made. **8th:** A normally happy Moon produces tensions. Do you overwork or do you feel lazy? Are you happy or anxious? Relax. **9th:** Are you bogged down by trivia, as usual? Do you forget the important? Try not to worry or you will get nothing done at all. **10th:** Concern for others may override your own problems, with positive results. **11th:** You can do everything, but do you want to? Eventually, it's exhausting.

12th: Are you so clever that you end up making blunders? Be a bit more communicative with your fountain of ideas.

HEAVENLY
RELATIONSHIPS

Those born in particular animal years may have
a close affinity with some animals and a positive
antipathy to others.

RATS are obsessive about sex and
can form intense sexual
relationships with Dragons,
and more long-lasting ones with
Pigs or Oxen. Galloping Horses and capricious Monkeys
prove too superficial, even though the initial attraction is
favourable.

OXEN can be similarly obsessive, but about companionship and well-balanced relationships. Roosters and
Dragons can fulfil this wish, with Tigers and Pigs proving
too aggressive.

TIGERS are intense and, surprisingly, passive, but can be unfaithful. Fellow Tigers make for a good balance, whilst the nervous Pig guarantees love will soon fritter away.

RABBITS are particularly fertile and can be teasers. A Mouse or Ox can cope and will prove a good partner. A Snake will devour the Rabbit emotionally and fellow Rabbits prove far too elusive for a relationship to blossom.

DRAGONS need lots of love and affection. A Rooster can be the perfect partner, with the opposite character of the Tiger curiously compatible; a genuine attraction of opposites. The devious Horse is best avoided and a Dog will prove disasterous for a long list of reasons.

SNAKES are warm and passive, needing the effusive Dragon or the considerate Dog as a good partner. With the Rat, Snakes get a taste of their own medicine, being gobbled up emotionally. A Tiger might appear attractive, but betrayal will be in the air.

HORSES, with their independent spirit, don't care for love. They might be attracted by the extrovert Tiger or flamboyant Dragon, but can expect nothing other than disaster with a Ram or the restless Monkey.

RAMS are cautious and become intimate very slowly. A lively Horse might break through the reserve, whilst a fellow Ram could offer real togetherness. A Rat could create an impression of an emotional relationship, but both signs would be fooling each other. An Ox is altogether too passive.

MONKEYS are restless and hyperactive. An Ox can tolerate this behaviour, with a Rat having a calming effect, bringing a whiff of domesticity. Tigers simply do not understand the Monkey's behaviour. The Horse may seem a perfect partner with matching energy, but eventually both partners will exhaust themselves.

ROOSTERS are alert and impatient, needing the good nature of a Pig to cope with what can often seem like aggression. A fellow Rooster can be difficult, fighting fiercely at first, but becoming devoted with the passage of time. A Dog will seem distant for the wide-awake Rooster, and a Rabbit, seemingly a good choice, will soon react with agression.

DOGS, whilst very sociable, are also loyal over the long-term. They can have passionate affairs with Tigers, through mutual respect despite seeming opposites. Pigs can prove the best long-lasting and loving partners. The nervy Mouse aggravates and the stubborn Ox soon ensures a battle of wills.

PIGS are contented with life, prepared to take things day-by-day. Rabbits can inject a bit of fun into a relationship and Dragons can be calmed down, ready to sit back and enjoy a quiet life. Snakes are totally unable to communicate with Pigs and a Horse will give the bumpiest ride.

HEAVENLY HEALTH

The year of birth can provide only a very general guide to symptoms to watch out for. It can't possibly cover all eventualities, especially unpleasant surprises. Take professional advice.

If you were born in the Year of the RAT, self-reliance can produce stress and a hectic social life can bring an unhealthy diet. Watch the canapés and that last glass of wine. OXEN can over-eat, munching their way through all manner of sweet things. Extremes of temperature can cause stomach and chest problems. TIGERS take on far too much and race ahead, not noticing symptoms, particularly strain, through over-confidence. RABBITS generally cossett themselves with lotions and potions, but for appearances, rather than health. Being homebodies, upheavals at home or work can cause illness. DRAGONS enjoy better health than most, but their extremes of temper bring stress and their dedication can lead to mild addiction. SNAKES are extremely sensitive to changes, of place or weather. They need a good night's sleep and should avoid any excess of activity, food or drink. HORSES are active and generally in good shape, but over-confidence in their condition can lead to strain on the lungs. Stop galloping. RAMS, too, are generally healthy, but should exercise with discretion. A little, done properly, will produce better results than frenzied aerobics. MONKEYS are endlessly agile, with a child-like delight in over-indulgence. They are easily tempted by any little luxury. Hold back. ROOSTERS, too, are restless and tend to over-indulge, not knowing when to stop, be it eating, working or sunbathing. Don't burn out. DOGS are robust, but take risks. A car crash is as bad for your health as too much alcohol. PIGS, seemingly powerful, are suprisingly delicate. Stomach and skin problems are common.

ANIMAL YEAR AND MOON MONTH CALCULATION CHART

YEAR	ANIMAL	1ST	2ND	3RD	4TH	5TH	6TH	7TH	8TH	9TH	10TH	11TH	12TH
1936	RAT	24.1	23.2	23.3	21.5	19.6	18.7	17.8	16.9	15.10	14.11	14.12	13.1.37
1937	OX	11.2	13.3	11.4	10.5	9.6	8.7	6.8	5.9	4.10	3.11	3.12	2.1.38
1938	TIGER	31.1	2.3	1.4	30.4	29.5	28.6	27.7	24.9	23.10	22.11	22.12	20.1.39
1939	RABBIT	19.2	21.3	20.4	19.5	17.6	17.7	15.8	13.9	13.10	11.11	11.12	9.1.40
1940	DRAGON	8.2	9.3	8.4	7.5	6.6	7.5	4.8	2.9	1.10	31.10	29.11	29.12
1941	SNAKE	27.1	26.2	28.3	26.4	26.5	25.6	23.8	21.9	20.10	19.11	18.12	17.1.42
1942	HORSE	15.2	17.3	15.4	15.5	14.6	13.7	12.8	10.9	10.10	8.11	8.12	6.1.43
1943	RAM	5.2	6.3	5.4	4.5	3.6	2.7	1.8	31.8	29.9	29.10	27.11	27.12
1944	MONKEY	25.1	24.2	24.3	23.4	21.6	20.7	19.8	17.9	17.10	16.11	15.12	14.1.45
1945	ROOSTER	13.2	14.3	12.4	12.5	10.6	9.7	8.8	6.9	6.10	5.11	5.12	3.1.46
1946	DOG	2.2	4.3	2.4	1.5	31.5	29.6	28.7	27.8	25.9	25.10	24.11	23.12
1947	PIG	22.1	21.2	21.4	20.5	19.6	18.7	16.8	15.9	14.10	13.11	12.12	11.11.48
1948	RAT	10.2	11.3	9.4	9.5	7.6	7.7	5.8	3.9	3.10	1.11	1.12	30.12
1949	OX	29.1	28.2	29.3	28.4	28.5	26.6	26.7	22.9	22.10	20.11	20.12	18.1.50
1950	TIGER	17.2	18.3	17.4	17.5	15.6	15.7	14.8	12.9	11.10	10.11	9.12	8.1.51
1951	RABBIT	6.2	8.3	6.4	6.5	5.6	4.7	3.8	1.9	1.10	30.10	29.11	28.12

Year	Animal												
1952	DRAGON	27.1	25.2	26.3	24.4	24.5	22.7	20.8	19.9	19.10	17.11	17.12	15.1.53
1953	SNAKE	14.2	15.3	14.4	13.5	11.6	11.7	10.8	8.9	8.10	7.11	6.12	5.1.54
1954	HORSE	3.2	5.3	3.4	3.5	1.6	30.6	30.7	28.8	27.9	27.10	25.11	25.12
1955	RAM	24.1	22.2	24.3	22.5	20.6	19.7	18.8	16.9	16.10	14.11	14.12	13.1.56
1956	MONKEY	12.2	12.3	11.4	10.5	9.6	8.7	6.8	5.9	4.10	3.11	2.12	1.1.57
1957	ROOSTER	31.1	2.3	31.3	30.4	29.5	28.6	27.7	25.8	23.9	23.10	22.11	21.12 20.1.58
1958	DOG	18.2	20.3	19.4	19.5	17.6	17.7	15.8	13.9	13.10	11.11	11.12	9.1.59
1959	PIG	8.2	9.3	8.4	8.5	6.6	6.7	4.8	3.9	2.10	1.11	30.11	30.12
1960	RAT	28.1	27.2	27.3	26.4	25.5	24.6	22.8	21.9	20.10	19.11	18.12	17.1.61
1961	OX	15.2	17.3	15.4	15.5	13.6	13.7	11.8	10.9	10.10	8.11	8.12	6.1.62
1962	TIGER	5.2	6.3	5.4	4.5	2.6	2.7	31.7	30.8	29.9	28.10	27.11	27.12
1963	RABBIT	25.1	24.2	25.3	24.4	21.6	21.7	19.8	18.9	17.10	16.11	16.12	15.1.64
1964	DRAGON	13.2	14.3	12.4	12.5	10.6	9.7	8.8	6.9	6.10	4.11	4.12	3.1.65
1965	SNAKE	2.2	3.3	2.4	1.5	31.5	29.6	28.7	27.8	25.9	24.10	23.11	23.12
1966	HORSE	21.1	20.2	22.3	20.5	19.6	18.7	16.8	15.9	14.10	12.11	12.12	11.1.67
1967	RAM	9.2	11.3	10.4	9.5	8.6	8.7	6.8	4.9	4.10	2.11	2.12	31.12
1968	MONKEY	30.1	28.2	29.3	27.4	27.5	26.6	25.7	22.9	22.10	20.11	20.12	18.1.69

YEAR	ANIMAL	1ST	2ND	3RD	4TH	5TH	6TH	7TH	8TH	9TH	10TH	11TH	12TH
1969	ROOSTER	17.2	18.3	17.4	16.5	15.6	14.7	13.8	12.9	11.10	10.11	9.12	8.1.70
1970	DOG	6.2	8.3	6.4	5.5	4.6	3.7	2.8	1.9	30.9	30.10	29.11	28.12
1971	PIG	27.1	25.5	27.3	25.4	24.5	22.7	21.8	19.9	19.10	18.11	18.12	16.1.72
1972	RAT	15.2	15.3	14.4	13.5	11.6	11.7	9.8	8.9	7.10	6.11	6.12	4.1.73
1973	OX	3.2	5.3	3.4	3.5	1.6	30.6	30.7	28.8	26.9	26.10	25.11	24.12
1974	TIGER	23.1	22.2	24.3	22.4	20.6	19.7	18.8	16.9	15.10	14.11	14.12	21.1.75
1975	RABBIT	11.2	13.3	12.4	11.5	10.6	9.7	7.8	6.9	5.10	3.11	3.12	1.1.76
1976	DRAGON	31.1	1.3	31.3	29.4	29.5	27.6	27.7	25.8	23.10	21.11	21.12	19.1.77
1977	SNAKE	18.2	20.3	18.4	18.5	17.6	16.7	15.8	13.9	13.10	11.11	11.12	9.1.78
1978	HORSE	7.2	9.3	7.4	7.5	6.6	5.7	4.8	3.9	2.10	1.11	30.11	30.12
1979	RAM	28.1	27.2	28.3	26.4	26.5	24.6	23.8	21.9	21.10	20.11	19.12	18.1.80
1980	MONKEY	16.2	17.3	15.4	14.5	13.6	12.7	11.8	9.9	9.10	8.11	7.12	6.1.81
1981	ROOSTER	5.2	6.3	5.4	4.5	2.6	2.7	31.7	29.8	28.9	28.10	26.11	26.12
1982	DOG	25.1	24.2	25.3	24.4	21.6	21.7	19.8	17.9	17.10	15.11	15.12	14.1.83
1983	PIG	13.2	15.3	13.4	13.5	11.6	10.7	9.8	7.9	6.10	5.11	4.12	3.1.84
1984	RAT	2.2	3.3	1.4	1.5	31.5	29.6	28.7	27.8	25.9	24.10	22.12	21.1.85

Year	Animal	1	2	3	4	5	6	7	8	9	10	11	12
1985	OX	20.2	21.3	20.4	20.5	18.6	18.7	16.8	15.9	14.10	12.11	12.12	10.1.86
1986	TIGER	9.2	10.3	9.4	9.5	7.6	7.7	6.8	4.9	4.10	2.11	2.12	31.12
1987	RABBIT	29.1	28.2	29.3	28.4	27.5	26.6	24.8	23.9	23.10	21.11	21.12	19.1.88
1988	DRAGON	17.2	18.3	16.4	16.5	14.6	14.7	12.8	11.9	11.10	9.11	9.12	8.1.89
1989	SNAKE	6.2	8.3	6.4	5.5	4.6	3.7	2.8	31.8	30.9	29.10	28.11	28.12
1990	HORSE	27.1	25.2	27.3	25.4	24.5	22.7	20.8	19.9	18.10	17.11	17.12	16.1.91
1991	RAM	15.2	16.3	15.4	14.5	12.6	12.7	10.8	8.9	8.10	6.11	6.12	5.1.92
1992	MONKEY	4.2	4.3	3.4	3.5	1.6	30.6	30.7	28.8	26.9	26.10	24.11	24.12
1993	ROOSTER	23.1	21.2	23.3	21.5	20.6	19.7	18.8	16.9	15.10	14.11	13.12	12.1.94
1994	DOG	10.2	12.3	11.4	11.5	9.6	9.7	7.8	6.9	5.10	3.11	3.12	1.1.95
1995	PIG	31.1	1.3	31.3	30.4	29.5	28.6	27.7	26.8	24.10	22.11	22.12	20.1.96
1996	RAT	19.2	19.3	18.4	17.5	16.6	16.7	14.8	13.9	12.10	11.11	11.12	9.1.97
1997	OX	7.2	9.3	7.4	7.5	5.6	5.7	3.8	2.9	2.10	31.10	30.11	30.12
1998	TIGER	28.1	27.2	28.3	26.4	26.5	23.7	22.8	21.9	20.10	19.11	19.12	17.1.99
1999	RABBIT	16.2	18.3	16.4	15.5	14.6	13.7	11.8	10.9	9.10	8.11	8.12	7.1.00
2000	DRAGON	5.2	6.3	5.4	4.5	2.6	2.7	31.7	29.8	28.9	27.10	26.11	26.12
2001	SNAKE	24.1	23.2	25.3	23.4	21.6	21.7	19.8	17.9	17.10	15.11	15.12	13.1.02

ACKNOWLEDGMENTS

Illustrations are from the Metropolitan Museum, New York,
the National Museum of Korea, the National Gallery, Prague,
the British Museum, London, the National Palace Museum,
Taipei, the Fine Art Gallery, San Diego, the Corcoran
Collection and Graparchive.

The publishers have made every effort to identify all
illustration sources. Any errors and omissions will be
corrected in future editions.